ARTIFICIAL INTELLIGENCE IN SMART HEALTH CARE SYSTEM

Y. JAHNAVI & P. NAGENDRA KUMAR

Made with ♥ on the Notion Press Platform
www.notionpress.com

Dedicated to

the divine lotus feet of

Sri Venkateswara

Contents

CHAPTER ONE

Introduction

The ever-increasing advancement in communication technologies of modern smart objects brings with it a new era of application development for Internet of Things (IoT) - based networks. This book proposes a standard model for the application of the Internet of Things and Artificial Intelligence in healthcare systems brings into light the existing literature and illustrates their contribution to different aspects of IoT. The IoT has a variety of application domains, including health care. The IoT revolution is redesigning modern health care with promising technological, economic, and social prospects. This book survey advances in IoT-based health care technologies and reviews the state-of-the-art network architectures/ platforms, applications, and industrial trends in IoT-based health care solutions. The IoT uses sensors to monitor the patients' health and collect data from patients, transfer these data to Machine learning for extraction, classification, and mining and use the pure data for prediction of the diseases. This article reflects the different branches of internet technology that can be used in the healthcare department i.e., the introduction of information technology, internet of things, computer network, and information technology are illustrated. Introduction to healthcare and HIT (healthcare information technology) and the introduction of the internet of things in the healthcare department along with its application and technology optimized with it in the present-day scenario.

The terms "information technology" and "IT" are widely used in business and the field of computing. People use the terms generically when referring to various kinds of computer-related work, which sometimes confuses their meaning. Information technology, according to a 1958 article in Harvard Business Review, consists of three basic components: numerical data processing, decision support, and business software.

This period saw the emergence of information technology as a formally organized area of business; in reality. Many businesses developed so-called "IT departments" to handle computer technology relevant to their operations over the following decades. Whatever these departments operated on became the de facto definition of information technology, which has developed over time. Computer tech support, enterprise computer network and database management, business software deployment, and information security are all duties of IT departments today. Especially during the dot-com boom of the 1990s, Information Technology also became associated with aspects of computing beyond those owned by IT departments. This wide-ranging definition of IT includes ranges like software development, computer systems architecture, and project management. One of the branches of information technology is IoT (the internet of things). The Internet of Things (IoT) is a term that encompasses everyone, everything, at any time, in any place, with any service, on any network. Many medical applications, such as remote health tracking, exercise programs, chronic diseases, and elderly care, may be enabled by the Internet of Things. Another significant possible application is compliance with treatment and medication at home and by healthcare providers. As a result, medical equipment, sensors, and diagnostic and imaging devices may all be considered smart devices or items that are integral to the IoT. Healthcare systems based on the Internet of Things are expected to lower costs, improve quality of life, and enhance the customer experience. In terms of healthcare providers, the Internet of Things has the ability to minimize system downtime by remote monitoring.

.INTERNET OF THINGS

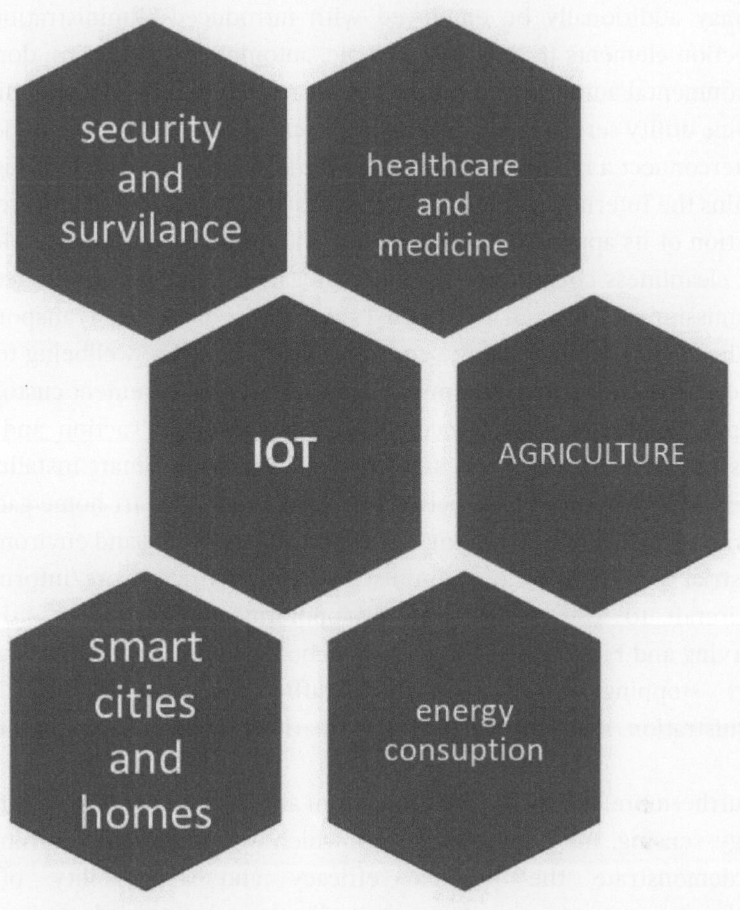

Figure 1: IoT Can Be Viewed as a Network of Networks

The Internet of Things (IoT) is a new concept that allows electronic devices and sensors to communicate with each other over the internet to make our lives easier. Smart devices and the internet are used by IoT to provide creative solutions to a variety of problems and issues faced by businesses, governments, and public/private industries all over the world. The Internet of Things (IoT) is becoming an increasingly important part of our lives, and it can be felt all around us. IoT is a technology that brings together a wide range of smart systems, structures, intelligent devices, and sensors. IoT gadgets are now not presently strongly standardized in how they are linked to the Internet, aside from their networking protocols. IoT may additionally be employed with introduced administration and protection elements to link, for example, automobile electronics, domestic environmental administration systems, smartphone networks, and manage of home utility services. The increasing scope of IoT and how it can be used to interconnect a range of disparate networks are proven in Fig. 1. Figure 1 explains the Internet of things is an idea that can be applied to any area. See a portion of its applications/models in various areas: Healthcare - Monitor hand cleanliness consistency through IoT gadgets and sensors to decrease transmission of Hospital Acquired Infections to patients, Transport and coordinations - Monitoring the coordination of vehicles' wellbeing to send cautions, Retail - Remote communication with items increment customized shopping experience, Insurance - Tracking customers' action and offer limits or prizes for solid and safe-conduct, Banking - Smart installments, Space - MARS Rover, Construction and Real Estate - Smart home gadgets/ locks/camera/security, Farming - Tracking soil wellbeing and environment, Industrial web - Smart Fleet administration and more sensors/information in Aircraft to keep away from disappointments, Wearables - Health observing and Fitness following. Savvy school, Infrastructure, for example, Smart stopping, Smart lighting, Traffic blockage, Hotels, Waste administration, and National security. Nearly it tends to be applied to any area.

Furthermore, it benefits from quantum and nanotechnology in terms of energy, sensing, and processing speed, which were previously unthinkable. To demonstrate the possible efficacy and applicability of IoT transformations, extensive research studies have been conducted and are available in the form of scientific papers, and press releases, both on the internet and in the form of printed materials. It could be used as a pre-work before developing novel creative business strategies that take security, assurance, and interoperability into account. The impact of the Internet already has had on education, communication, business, science, government, and humanity. Clearly, the Internet is one of the most important and powerful creations in all of human history. Now consider that IoT represents the next evolution of the Internet, taking a huge leap in its ability to gather, analyze, and distribute data that we can turn into information, knowledge, and, ultimately, wisdom. In this context, IoT becomes immensely important. Already, IoT projects are underway that promise to close the gap between poor and rich, improve the distribution of the world's resources to those who need them most, and help us understand our planet so we can be more proactive and less reactive. Even so, several barriers exist that threaten to slow IoT development, including the transition to IPv6, having a common set of standards, and developing energy sources for millions—even billions—of minute sensors.

CHAPTER TWO

IOT as a Network of Networks

Presently, IoT is comprised of a free assortment of different, reason assembled networks. The present vehicles, for instance, have numerous organizations to control motor capacity, security highlights, interchanges frameworks, etc. Business and private structures additionally have different control frameworks for warming, venting, and cooling (HVAC); telephone utility; security; and lighting. As IoT develops, these organizations, and numerous others, will be associated with added security, examination, and board capacities. This will permit IoT to turn out to be considerably more remarkable in what it can help individuals accomplish.

COMPUTER NETWORKING AND INFORMATION TECHNOLOGY

Company computer networking issues are mostly synonymous with Information Technology because networks play such an important role in the activity of many businesses. The following are some networking patterns that are important in IT:

- Since networks play such an important role in the operations of many companies, company computer networking problems are often confused with information technology.
- The following are some significant networking trends in IT. Quality and power of the network: The popularity of online video has resulted in a significant increase in network bandwidth demand, both on the Internet and within IT networks. New types of software applications that embrace richer graphics and deeper interaction with computers tend to produce more data and thereby increase network traffic.
- Mobile and wireless usages: In addition to standard PCs and workstations, IT network administrators now have to accommodate a

wide range of smartphones and tablets. High-performance wireless hotspots with roaming capabilities are popular in IT environments. Deployments in larger office buildings are meticulously designed and checked to avoid dead spots and signal interference. Cloud services: While in the past, IT shops had their own server farms for hosting email and business databases, others have moved to cloud storage environments, where the data is managed by third-party hosting providers. This shift in computing models has a major impact on traffic patterns on a company network, but it also necessitates a significant investment in employee training.

CHAPTER THREE

IoT in HEALTH CARE

Healthcare is an important factor in life. Unfortunately, the rapidly aging population, coupled with the increase in chronic disease, is putting tremendous pressure on current healthcare systems, with a high demand for anything from hospital beds to doctors and nurses. Clearly, a solution is needed to relieve the strain on healthcare systems while maintaining high-quality care for at-risk patients. Much recent research has focused on the Internet of Things (IoT), which has been widely described as a possible solution to relieve the burdens on healthcare systems. A significant portion of this study focuses on patient monitoring for specific disorders like diabetes or Parkinson's disease. Further research is being conducted with the aim of serving particular goals, such as assisting recovery by continuously tracking a patient's progress. Similar works have also described emergency healthcare as a possibility, but it has not yet been thoroughly investigated. Several previous studies have looked at particular areas and developments related to IoT in healthcare and presented a comprehensive survey with a focus on commercially available solutions, potential implementations, and unsolved issues. Rather than being discussed as part of a broader context, each subject is examined on its own. Data mining, storage, and analysis, but there is no mention of their incorporation into a system that compares sensor styles, with a particular emphasis on communications. However, drawing a picture of a complete system from this book is difficult. Finally, sensing and big data management are considered, but the network that will enable communications is ignored.

This book contributes to the field by identifying all main components of an end-to-end Internet of Things healthcare system and proposing a general model that can be extended to all IoT-based healthcare systems. This is important since there are currently no end-to-end systems for remote health monitoring in the literature. This book also includes a thorough examination of the current state-of-the-art innovations that come under the proposed model. Sensors for tracking different health criteria, short- and long-range communication standards, and cloud technology are all being studied. This book differs from previous major survey contributions in that it considers each critical component of an IoT-based healthcare system both individually and as a whole. By focusing on something new, you will make an even more original contribution.

Overview of IoT in the Healthcare System

Medical care is one of the quickest growing business sectors of the present economy; more individuals require care, and it is getting all the more exorbitant. Government consumption on medical care has hit an unequalled pinnacle, while the fundamental requirement for improved patient-physicist ties has become visible. Technologies, for example, large information and fake learning can give the two licenses and suppliers of improved therapy and diminished expenses. Various organizations and associations have effectively ventured out in this field. Which elevated the change to patient and proof based consideration. The information is there; we simply need to work out how to see it. In expansion, the learning of the framework relies generally upon the information and calculations accessible to sort information in specific classes through regulated learning or unregulated learning. Individuals take wrong choices and here and there we people depend on realities to make any move. The decision we make frequently incorporates feeling, yet machines will not. We people can choose dependent on our good qualities, our worldwide perception, political and strict worth, and our personality. The information assortment accessible to prepare PCs for dynamic will incorporate these variables. These elements It is additionally a test to guarantee that the information assortment used to gain is liberated from hardware so particularly far as conceivable human biases. Beating IoT and ML shortcomings will build the soundness of the customer more. This chapter centered to examine the overall view on IoT and ML which are applied in the medical care framework, the application utilized for customized medical services and exhibited some other related works and their sentiments

The suitability of upcoming licensed-band standards, such as NB-IoT, to competing for unlicensed-band standards is contrasted, with a focus on healthcare applications. The rest of the book contains the area of the Internet of Things, focusing on the provision of services.

HEALTH INFORMATION TECHNOLOGY (HIT)

Health information technology (HIT) is the use of computer hardware and software to store, retrieve, share, and use health care information, data, and expertise for communication and decision making. Computers and communications attributes that can be networked to create networks for moving health information are referred to as HIT.

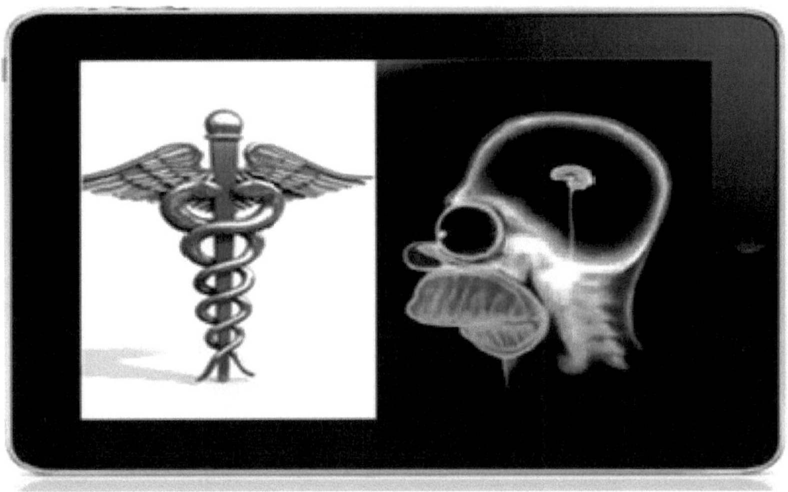

Figure 2: Health Information Systems

With the rise of computers in the early 1950s, the worldwide use of computer technology in medicine began. Gustav Wagner founded Germany's first professional association for health informatics in 1949. Health informatics, also known as Health Information Systems, is a field that combines information technology, computer science, and medicine (Fig 2). Figure 2 elaborates that "the application of information processing involving both computer hardware and software that deals with the storage, retrieval, sharing, and use of health care information, health data, and knowledge for communication and decision making". It is concerned with the tools, software, and methods needed to optimize information collection, storage, retrieval, and use in health and biomedicine.

Computers, clinical protocols, standardized medical terminologies, and information and communication systems are all examples of health informatics methods. Nursing, clinical care, dentistry, pharmacy, public health, occupational therapy, and (bio) medical studies are some of the fields in which it is used. During the 1960s, France, Germany, Belgium, and the Netherlands developed specialized university departments and Informatics training programs. Medical informatics research units first appeared in Poland and the United States in the 1970s. Since then, the United States, the European Union, and several developing countries have worked to improve high-quality health informatics science, education, and infrastructure.

Medical education has changed dramatically around the world as a result of technological advancements. The majority of medical students are now computer literate, which is a significant improvement. New medical knowledge is readily available on the Internet and via portable computers such as palmtops and personal digital assistants (PDA). Information technology, such as college networks and the internet, can help medical education in a variety of ways. Some solutions include computer-assisted learning (CAL), virtual reality (VR), and human patient simulators. Medical students and teachers can communicate even when they are not in school thanks to college networks and the Internet.

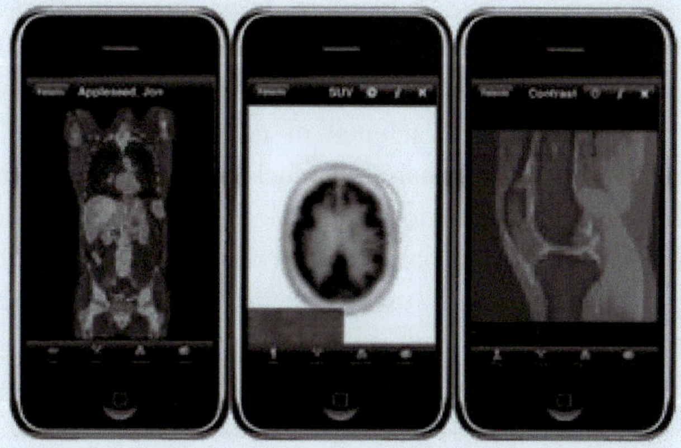

Figure 3: Image Processing Technology

E-mails can be used to create rapid contact, and course information, handouts, and reviews can be easily distributed. To highlight and organize their courses, many medical schools now use online services such as "Blackboard" or "student central." Tutors, assessors, and students at any site may look at the curricular background of their own individual contributions using such programs, which allow for easy access to information and quick turnaround on assessment and messaging. Similarly, the Internet allows users to obtain up-to-date information on various aspects of health and disease, as well as communicate with colleagues across continents through net conferencing. Medline, numerous medical journals, online textbooks, and the most up-to-date information on current developments in medicine are all available for free, which promotes learning and study.

CAL is regarded as a fun way to learn and is particularly well suited to conceptually challenging topics. Histopathology, anatomy, and heart sounds are all studied using interactive digital materials. The use of computed tomography and magnetic resonance imaging to create anatomical three-dimensional atlases of different internal organs is very instructive and helps students understand (fig. 3). The list number of diseases that can be interpreted using (figure 3 elaborates) image processing technologies starting from 2D images up to complex four dimensional Doppler images. Two-dimension images like x-ray images like tuberculosis, lung disorders emphysema, pneumonia, etc., can be easily collected and processed. These chest disorders can be graded and formatting tree according to Indian patterns. The various bone disorders like cervical spondylosis, bony fractures, malignancies, and subclinical bone material changes can be assessed and processed.

Another advancement is the use of "Advanced Life Support" (ACLS) simulators and Haptics "the science of contact" simulators in medical education for practicing clinical skills such as ECG perception, effective action such as ABC, medications, injections, and defibrillation without having to operate on a real patient. In today's modern medical schools, technologically sophisticated "virtual reality" simulators with advanced medical simulation technology and medical databases are available to introduce medical students to a wide variety of complicated medical situations. It may mimic a variety of clinical procedures including catheterization, laparoscopy, and bronchoscopy, among others. Students can digitally go inside each organ to see how it looks from the outside as well as the inside thanks to modern technology.

The healthcare industry has benefited greatly from information technology. The introduction of electronic medical records is one example of a major improvement that IT has brought to hospitals (EMR). This technology will combine several databases of medical data into a single database. Not only does this technology save money on paper, but it also saves time, With the click of a button, healthcare professionals can access vital patient details such as medical history, prescriptions, insurance information, and more.

In the clinical setting, EMRs hold a lot of promise. The ability to care for patients with a record that is integrated with laboratory that pharmacy data and offers point-of-service information on preventive procedures, diagnosis, treatment, and follow-up is a significant step forward in-patientcare. If all clinicians used EMRs, improving and assessing quality would be much easier. It would be simple to warn clinicians that their diabetic patient requires an eye examination or a haemoglobin A1C amount.

Individual clinicians‘ drug prescribing habits may be scrutinized and compared to defined benchmarks. Indeed, computer-assisted clinical support as part of an EMR has been shown to improve physician productivity and patient outcomes.

Medical error reduction has been a top priority all over the world. Adverse drug reactions, in particular, are a common cause of injury in hospitalized patients. Computerized physician order entry (CPOE) systems have become more popular as a result of the need to increase patient safety. CPOE systems, in general, require physicians to write all orders electronically. These systems have the ability to verify that written instructions are accurate, that is, they can confirm the dosage and contraindications of a given medication based on a patient profile. They have been shown to minimize severe drug errors significantly.

Computerized provider order entry (CPOE), formerly known as Computer physician order entry, has been shown to minimize overall prescription error rates by 80% and adverse (harmful to the patient) errors by 55%. According to a Leapfrog survey from 2004, 16 percent of US clinics, hospitals, and medical practices are required to use CPOE within two years. According to a recent report, CPOE adoption decreased drug errors, and if broadly adopted, CPOE might significantly reduce the annual number of those errors. A standardized bar code system for dispensing medications, in addition to electronic prescribing, could eliminate a quarter of medication errors. Other error-proofing steps include providing consumers with information about the drugs' risks and improving medication packaging (clear labelling, avoiding similar drug names, and including dose reminders).

The impact of technology on medicine and education is undeniable. However, there are still many areas that need to be changed before we can fully use IT. Last but not least, no matter how sophisticated technology becomes, it will never be able to substitute the contact that doctors and students need with patients, as well as the professional decisions that distinguish great doctors. As a result, in our pursuit of new technology, we must be careful not to ignore the doctor-patient relationship.

INTERNET OF THINGS AND HEALTHCARE

Healthcare's focus on IoT is growing by the day in order to expand access to care, raise quality, and, most significantly, lower costs. The comprehensive practice of well-being, healthcare, and patient support is referred to as personalized healthcare because it is based on an individual's particular biological, behavioural, social, and cultural characteristics. This empowers each and every citizen by adhering to the fundamental healthcare concept of "the right treatment for the right person at the right time," which contributes to improved outcomes and satisfaction, as well as cost-effective healthcare. Instead of costly clinical treatment, a sustainable service focuses on prevention, early pathology detection, and homecare, and monitors general well-being to anticipate needs and ensure compliance with healthcare plans. The Internet of Things aims to personalize care facilities and give each consumer a digital identity. The Internet of Things aims to control the personalization of care services and to provide each user with a digital identity. In healthcare, various equipment is used to communicate and create the ubiquitous system-of-system. IoT-based personalization classifications. The classifications of IoT based personalized healthcare systems are Clinical care and remote monitoring.

CHAPTER FOUR

APPLICATIONS OF INTERNET OF THINGS IN HEALTHCARE

Healthcare industry devices that are part of an intelligent system provide better care by automating procedures, encouraging cooperation, and securely managing information. From in-home monitoring devices to massive hospital-based imaging systems and thin-client solutions, healthcare industry devices that are part of an intelligent system offer better care by automating processes, facilitating communication, and securely managing information. Intelligent networks make it easier for physicians to access health information, reduce costs, and increase operational efficiencies, all of which contribute to a better patient experience. The following are some examples.

1. **Monitor an elderly family member**: Fortunately, technology may help caregivers, healthcare professionals, or family members detect and warn caregivers, healthcare professionals, or family members of changes in an elderly person's actions, which can help avoid serious issues. The Internet of Things is uniquely placed among the technologies available to allow caregivers to help the well-being of those at risk while others cannot. IoT-enabled monitors minimize emergency hospital admissions and encourage elders to comfortably remain in their homes longer by monitoring key health indicators such as dehydration and malnutrition, as well as behavioural changes such as decreased mobility.
2. **Scalable, continuous, heart rate monitoring:** Photoplethysmography (PPG) is a low-cost optical technique for detecting volumetric changes

in blood flowing through capillaries at the skin's surface. In the late 1800s, scientists developed photoplethysmography, which enabled them to observe real-time blood flow using light bulbs. The word photoplethysmography was invented by scientists in the late 1930s. PPG's technologies now concentrate on consumer applications using wearable devices, thanks to technological advancements. The effects of these wearable devices are normally interpreted using a peripheral unit. Smartphones have largely replaced such peripheral devices in terms of delivering data to users in a user-friendly manner. Bluetooth technology is used to connect to mobile phones. Bluetooth is a low-power wireless communication technology that allows two compatible devices to link, send, and receive data over the air.

Photoplethysmography is a form of plethysmography that uses a simple optical setup to detect changes in peripheral blood circulation volume. Since measurements are taken at the skin's surface, this procedure is non-invasive. The technology illuminates' the skin with optoelectronic components like a red or near-infrared light source and a photodetector that detects variations in light intensity within the observed region. To illuminate skin, a red or near-infrared source of light is usually used. This light then passes through tissues, where pigments, bones, and blood absorb it. The PPG sensors look at the world through an optical lens change in blood flow volume by detecting changes in light intensity.

1. **The communication procedures of the proposed IOT-based healthcare system:** In the proposed IoT-based healthcare system, we consider that a nurse with his/her intelligent devices (acting as a local processing unit) would like to provide on-demand patient care services via an automatic and contactless data retrieval mechanism. As the IoT communication network is public, a robust authentication procedure is required for secure data exchange among wearable bio-sensors, the local processing unit, and the BSN server.
2. **Benefits of Health Information Technology:** Electronic health records are also used by the majority of obstetrician-gynecologists. Because of the awareness of their potential benefits and government policies that incentivize their use, they have quickly gained traction. The ability to store and retrieve data, as well as the ability to quickly communicate patient information in a legible format, are all advantages of health

information technology (IT): improved drug protection through improved legibility, which can reduce the likelihood of medication errors; and the ease with which patient information can be retrieved. Medication warnings, health flags, and reminders improved monitoring and documentation of appointments and diagnostic tests, clinical decision support, and the availability of full patient data all have the potential to enhance patient safety. Data collected by the use of health information technology can be used to assess the effectiveness of treatment treatments and has been shown to enhance medical practice. Alerts will also ensure that standards and evidence-based care are followed. Record consistency can be structured to minimize procedure differences, perform quality assurance audits, and maximize proof. Patient interest as healthcare consumers is growing as a result of health information technology. It gives patients access to their medical records, making them more informed about their conditions and encouraging them to engage actively in joint decision-making. It may enhance follow-up with missed appointments, examinations, and diagnostic tests outside of the patient experience. Within a practice, a health care provider may look for particular cohorts of patients to track and increase adherence to recommended health care, such as mammograms, Pap tests, or hemoglobin A1c levels.

3. **Wearable devices:** Bracelets, pendants, buttons, smartwatches, t-shirts, intelligent rings, sneakers, exercise trackers, and other public health equipment, as well as portable systems, can all be worn on the human body. The wearable system in direct contact will monitor the disease, the individual's health, and the data collected from the central research center. Wearable technologies, such as sensing, computing, and displays, are three of the elements. Usable devices will produce biological data including calories burned, steps taken, heart rate, blood pressure, and exercise time, among other things. These devices have a significant impact, and there is a high likelihood that the customer's physical well-being will improve.

CHAPTER FIVE

Introduction to Machine Learning

Machine learning is an application of artificial intelligence (AI) that provides systems the ability to automatically learn and improve from experience without being explicitly programmed. Machine learning focuses on the development of computer programs that can access data and use it learn for themselves. The process of learning begins with observations or data, such as examples, direct experience, or instruction, in order to look for patterns in data and make better decisions in the future based on the examples that we provide. The primary aim is to allow the computers learn automatically without human intervention or assistance and adjust actions accordingly. But, using the classic algorithms of machine learning, text is considered as a sequence of keywords; instead, an approach based on semantic analysis mimics the human ability to understand the meaning of a text.

A lot has been said during the past several years about how precision medicine and, more concretely, how genetic testing is going to disrupt the way diseases like cancer are treated. Numerous malignant growth victims with a particular type and phase of most cancers for the most part was advised and got the equivalent treatment sooner than the presentation of personalized medication. In any case, it becomes certain that unique treatments worked preferable for explicit victims over for all the others. As a result of the exploration inside the genetics, scientists discovered that there are varieties in genetics of people thus in their tumours. Because of this, for specific victim the response to the treatment transformed into particular. Once sequenced, a disease tumour can have a huge number of genetic changes.

But the difficult task is to separate the mutations that are responsible for tumour growth from the neutral mutations. Not all mutations lead to cancer. Due to a mutation in a gene, there is some genetic variation developed in a gene. But the question comes, from which particular mutation this genetic variation happened in a gene. Right now, this understanding of genetic mutations is being done physically which is a very tedious assignment. Based on a gene and a variation in it, a clinical pathologist has to manually check and classify each and every single genetic mutation based on evidence from text-based clinical literature. Generally, a machine learning (ML) based predictive system in healthcare uses data (genetic profile or clinical parameters) and learning algorithms to predict target values for cancer detection.

CHAPTER SIX

Machine Learning Algorithms

Machine learning uses artificial intelligence and statistical techniques to let computers to learn progressively to improve performance on a specific task with data with or without being supervised. Within the field of data analytics, machine learning is a method used to devise complex models and algorithms that lend to prediction. It is also known as predictive analytics. These analytical models allow us to produce reliable, repeatable decisions and results and uncover hidden insights through learning from historical relationships and trends in the data. Depends on whether there is learning feedback available, machine learning is typically classified into two broad categories supervised and unsupervised learning. In our research the task is to classify genetic mutations to enable personized medicine for cancer treatment. Due to the nature of given dataset is text-based, a conversion is needed for any classification algorithms can adopted. Classification techniques which are widely used by researchers and hence selected as focus areas of study.

Accessing information has acquired greater magnitude in the current context of knowledge-based system. However, with the availability of broadband, access of information does not pose a problem. This age of information is experiencing an overwhelming proliferation of documents. The huge quantity of digitalized content has resulted in a dire need for the evolution of advanced and sophisticated techniques of Machine Learning. In spite of the extensive research conducted in this area, Machine Learning is still considered as an open research area. This is the source of motivation for the selection of Machine Learning for this work. There exists various Classification Algorithms in Machine Learning. The accuracy depends on the selection of classification algorithm. Sometimes all attributes may not be useful. Therefore, the removal of a few attributes from the dataset is required to improve the accuracy.

TYPES OF MACHINE LEARNING

There exist various types of machine learning such as supervised learning, unsupervised learning and reinforcement learning.

Supervised Learning

Supervised learning is one of the most basic types of machine learning. In this type, the machine learning algorithm is trained on labelled data. Even though the data needs to be labelled accurately for this method to work, supervised learning is extremely powerful when used in the right circumstances.

In supervised learning, the ML algorithm is given a small training dataset to work with. This training dataset is a smaller part of the bigger dataset and serves to give the algorithm a basic idea of the problem, solution, and data points to be dealt with. The training dataset is also very similar to the final dataset in its characteristics and provides the algorithm with the labelled parameters required for the problem.

The algorithm then finds relationships between the parameters given essentially establishing a cause-and-effect relationship between the variables in the dataset. At the end of the training, the algorithm has an idea of how the data works and the relationship between the input and the output.

This solution is then deployed for use with the final dataset, which it learns from in the same way as the training dataset. This means that supervised machine learning algorithms will continue to improve even after being deployed, discovering new patterns and relationships as it trains itself on new data.

Unsupervised Learning

Unsupervised machine learning holds the advantage of being able to work with unlabelled data. This means that human labour is not required to make the dataset machine-readable, allowing much larger datasets to be worked on by the program.

In supervised learning, the labels allow the algorithm to find the exact nature of the relationship between any two data points. However, unsupervised learning does not have labels to work off of, resulting in the creation of hidden structures. Relationships between data points are perceived by the algorithm in an abstract manner, with no input required from human beings.

The creation of these hidden structures is what makes unsupervised learning algorithms versatile. Instead of a defined and set problem statement, unsupervised learning algorithms can adapt to the data by dynamically changing hidden structures. This offers more post-deployment development than supervised learning algorithms.

Reinforcement Learning

Reinforcement learning techniques in organizations

Reinforcement learning directly takes inspiration from how human beings learn from data in their lives. It features an algorithm that improves upon itself and learns from new situations using a trial-and-error method. Favourable outputs are encouraged or 'reinforced', and non-favourable outputs are discouraged or 'punished'.

Based on the psychological concept of conditioning, reinforcement learning works by putting the algorithm in a work environment with an interpreter and a reward system. In every iteration of the algorithm, the output result is given to the interpreter, which decides whether the outcome is favourable or not.

In case of the program finding the correct solution, the interpreter reinforces the solution by providing a reward to the algorithm. If the outcome is not favourable, the algorithm is forced to reiterate until it finds a better result. In most cases, the reward system is directly tied to the effectiveness of the result.

In typical reinforcement learning use-cases, such as finding the shortest route between two points on a map, the solution is not an absolute value. Instead, it takes on a score of effectiveness, expressed in a percentage value. The higher this percentage value is, the more reward is given to the algorithm. Thus, the program is trained to give the best possible solution for the best possible reward.

2.2 DECISION TREE

A decision tree is a hierarchical data structure implementing the divide-and-conquer strategy. It is an efficient nonparametric method, which can be used for both classification and regression.

Learning algorithms can directly build the tree from a given labelled training sample. The tree can be converted to a set of simple rules that are easy to understand. Another possibility is to learn a rule base directly.

A decision tree is a hierarchical model for supervised learning whereby the local region is identified in a sequence of recursive splits in a smaller number of steps. A decision tree is composed of internal decision nodes and terminal leaves. Each decision node m implements a test function $f_m(x)$ with discrete outcomes labelling the branches. Given an input, at each node, a test is applied and one of the branches is taken depending on the outcome. This process starts at the root and is repeated recursively until a leaf node is hit, at which point the value written in the leaf constitutes the output.

A decision tree is a nonparametric model in the sense that were not assume any parametric form for the class densities. The tree structure is not fixed a priori but the tree grows, branches and leaves are added, during learning depending on the complexity of the problem inherent in the data.

Each $f_m(x)$ defines a discriminant in the d-dimensional input space dividing it into smaller regions that are further subdivided as we take a path from the root down.$f_m(\cdot)$ is a simple function and when written down as a tree, a complex function is broken down into a series of simple decisions. Different decision tree methods assume different models for $f_m(\cdot)$, and the model class defines the shape of the discriminant and the shape of regions. Each leaf node has an output label, which in the case of classification is the class code and in regression is a numeric value. A leaf node defines a localized region in the input space where instances falling in this region have the same labels (in classification), or very similar numeric outputs (in regression). The boundaries of the regions are defined by the discriminants that are coded in the internal nodes on the path from the root to the leaf node.

The hierarchical placement of decisions allows a fast localization of the region covering an input. For example, if the decisions are binary, then in the best case, each decision eliminates half of the cases. If there are b regions, then in the best case, the correct region can be found in log b decisions. Another advantage of the decision tree is interpretability. As we will see shortly, the tree can be converted to a set of IF-THEN rules that are easily understandable. For this reason, decision trees are very popular and sometimes preferred over more accurate but less interpretable methods.

There are two types of decision trees:

1. Univariate trees
2. Multivariate trees

During the late 1970's, a decision tree algorithm known as ID3 (Iterative Dichotomiser) was introduced. The successor of ID3 was C4.5. Then CART (Classification and Regression Trees) was invented. In all these algorithms decision trees are constructed in a top-down recursive divide and conquer manner.

ITERATIVE DICHOTOMISER (ID3)

ID3 was introduced by Quinlan for constructing the decision trees form database. In ID3, each node corresponds to a splitting attribute and each arc is a possible value of that attribute. At each node the splitting attribute is selected to be the most informative among the attributes not yet considered in the path from the root. Attribute selection methods are used for finding the goodness of the split.

C4.5 (J48)

C4.5 is an extension of ID3 that accounts for unavailable values, continuous attribute value rages, pruning of decision trees and rule derivation. In Weka, experimentation was done by using C4.5, which is named as J48. Unlike CART, which generates a binary decision tree, C4.5 produces trees with variable branches per node. When a discrete variable is chosen as the splitting attribute in C4.5, there will be one branch for each value of the attribute.

CART ALGORITHM:

Classification may refer to categorization, the process in which ideas and objects are recognized, differentiated and understood. An algorithm that implements classification, especially in a concrete implementation, is known as a classifier. The term “classifier” sometimes also refers to the mathematical function, implemented by a classification algorithm that maps input data to a category.

In the terminology of machine learning, classification is considered an instance of supervised learning, i.e., learning where a training set of correctly identified observations is available. The corresponding unsupervised procedure is unknown as clustering or cluster analysis, and involves grouping data into categories based on some measure of inherent similarity.

Classification algorithms in Machine Learning creates a step-by-step guide for how to determine the output of a decision must be made based on the input, and to move to the next node and then ext until one reach a leaf that tells the predicted output.

There is also some argument over whether classification methods that do not involve a statistical model can be considered “statistical”. Other fields may use different terminology: e.g., in community ecology, the term "classification" normally refers to cluster analysis, i.e., a type of unsupervised learning, rather than the supervised learning.

SIMPLE CART:

Simple Cart method is CART (Classification and Regression Tree) analysis. CART is abbreviated as Classification and Regression Tree algorithm. It was developed by Leo Breimanin the early 1980s. It is used for data exploration and prediction also. Classification and regression trees are classification methods which in order to construct decision trees uses historical data. CART uses learning sample which is a set of historical data with pre- assigned classes for all observations for building decision tree.

SimpleCart (Classification and regression tree) is a classification technique that generates the binary decision tree. Since output is binary tree, it generates only two children. Entropy is used to choose the best splitting attribute. Simple Cart handles the missing data by ignoring that record. This algorithm is best for the training data. Classification and regression trees (CART) decision tree is a learning technique, which gives the results as either classification or regression trees, depending on categorical or numeric data set.

The methodology proposed by is perhaps best known and most widely used. It uses cross-validation or a large independent test sample of data to select the best tree from the sequence of trees considered in the pruning process. The basic CART building algorithm is a greedy algorithm in that it chooses the locally best discriminatory feature at each stage in the process. This is suboptimal but a full search for a fully optimized set of question would be computationally very expensive. The CART approach is an alternative to the traditional methods for prediction. In the implementation of CART, the dataset is split into the two subgroups that are the most different with respect to the outcome. This procedure is continued on each subgroup until some minimum subgroup size is reached.

RANDOM TREE CLASSIFIERS:

Random Tree is a supervised Classifier; it is an ensemble learning algorithm that generates many individual learners. It employs a bagging idea to produce a random set of data for constructing a decision tree. In standard tree each node is split using the best split among all variables. In a random forest, each node is split using the best among the subset of predicators randomly chosen at that node.

Random trees have been introduced by Leo Breiman and Adele Cutler. The algorithm can deal with both classification and regression problems. Random trees are a collection (ensemble) of tree predictors that is called forest. The classification works as follows:

- The random trees classifier takes the input feature vector

- Classifies it with every tree in the forest
- Outputs the class label that received the majority of "votes".

In case of a regression, the classifier response is the average of the responses over all the trees in the forest. Random Trees are essentially the combination of two existing algorithms in Machine Learning: single model trees are combined with Random Forest ideas. Model trees are decision trees where every single leaf holds a linear model which is optimized for the local subspace described by this leaf. Random Forests have shown to improve the performance of single decision trees considerably: tree diversity is generated by two ways of randomization. First the training data is sampled with replacement for each single tree like in Bagging. Secondly, when growing a tree, instead of always computing the best possible split for each node only a random subset of all attributes is considered at every node, and the best split for that subset is computed. Such trees have been for classification Random model trees for the first time combine model trees and random forests. Random trees employ this produce for split selection and thus induce reasonably balanced trees where one global setting for the ridge value works across all leaves, thus simplifying the optimization procedure.

REPTree:

REPTree uses the regression tree logic and creates multiple trees in different iterations. After that it selects best one from all generated trees. That will be considered as the representative. In pruning the tree the measure used is the mean square error on the predictions made by the tree.

Basically, Reduced Error Pruning Tree ("REPTree") is fast decision tree learning and it builds a decision tree based on the information gain or reducing the variance. REP Tree is a fast decision tree learner which builds a decision or regression tree using information gain as the splitting criterion, and prunes it using reduced error pruning. It only sorts values for numeric attributes once.

Tree Pruning

The training data may contain noise and outliers. The decision tree constructed by using such data may contain anomalies. The branches with anomalies should be removed. Pruning is the technique used to remove the branches with anomalies. There are two types of pruning

i. Prepruning
ii. Postpruning

In Prepruning approach, a tree is pruned by halting its construction early, whereas in Postpruning approach, the subtrees are removed from a fully grown tree. No single pruning method has been found to be superior over others. Postpruning requires more computation than Prepruning. Postpruning produces more reliable tree.

Bayesian Classification

Bayesian classifiers are statistical classifiers. They can predict class membership probabilities, such as the probability that a given tuple belongs to particular class. Bayesian classification is based on Baye's theorem.

Classification by Backpropagation

Introduction to Neural Networks:

A Neural Networks is a machine that is designed to model the way in which the brain performs a particular task. Neural Networks are trained such that a particular input leads to a specified target output. Based on the comparison of the output and the target, the network is adjusted till the network output is close to the target

Network architecture:

The arrangement of neurons into layers and the pattern of connection within and in between layers are called as architecture of the network. There are various types of network architectures: single layer feed forward networks, multilayer feed forward networks, recurrent networks etc.

A single layer feed forward network has one layer of neurons. Single layer refers to the output layer of computation nodes or neurons. The input layer of source nodes is not counted because no computation is performed there. The inputs may be fully connected to the output units through weighted edges.

A multilayer feed forward network has one or more hidden layers of nodes between the input and output units. All neurons in the successive layers are connected with weighted edges. The signals flow from the input units to the output units via hidden layers. This type of network can be used to solve problems that are more complicated than linearly separable spaces.

A recurrent network can be distinguished from a feed forward neural network in one aspect, that it has at least one feedback loop.

Multilayer perceptron Neural Networks (MLPNN)

Multilayer perceptron Neural Networks is a class of neural networks which consists of a set of sensory units that constitute the input layer and one or more hidden layers of computation nodes and an output layer of computation nodes. A nonlinear activation function namely sigmoid function is widely used to generate output activation in the computation nodes. The task of MLPNN model development for an application involves two aspects- the first one being setting the weight parameters of the connecting edges and the second being identifying appropriate structure parameters. In general, MLP Neural Networks are trained with the back propagation algorithm for setting the weight parameters to develop classification and regression models in accordance with a set of known examples and hence comes under supervisory training.

Support Vector Machines

Support Vector Machine (SVM) is a potential technique for data classification. This technique uses a linear model to implement nonlinear class boundaries through some sort of nonlinear mapping of input vectors into a high dimensional feature space. SVM approach has been applied to several applications such as credit rating analysis, time series prediction insurance claim fraud detection etc., and the studies reported that SVM was comparable and even performed better than other classifiers like ANN, MDA, Logit etc.

An attempt was made to suggest a new bankruptcy prediction model with better explanatory power and stability using support vector machines. Performance of the developed model was compared with multiple discriminant analysis (MDA), logistic regression analysis and three layer fully connected back propagation neural networks and the results proved that SVM outperforms other methods.

Rule Based Classification

In this classifier, the learned model is represented as a set of IF-THEN rules. IF-THEN rules are generated either directly using sequential covering algorithm or from a decision tree. An IF-THEN rule is in the form of IF *condition* THEN *conclusion*.

Rule extraction from a Decision Tree:

To extract rules from a decision tree, one rule is created for each path from the root to a leaf node. Each splitting criterion along a given path is logically ANDed to form the rule antecedent. The leaf node contains the class prediction, forming the rule consequent.

Logistic Regression

This type of statistical analysis (also known as logit model) is often used for predictive analytics and modelling, and extends to applications in machine learning. In this analytics approach, the dependent variable is finite or categorical: either A or B (binary regression) or a range of finite options

A, B, C or D (multinomial regression). It is used in statistical software to understand the relationship between the dependent variable and one or more independent variables by estimating probabilities using a logistic regression equation.

This type of analysis can help you predict the likelihood of an event happening or a choice being made. Logistic regression is used in various fields, including machine learning, most medical fields, and social sciences.

Stacking Model Classification

Stacking or Stacked Generalization is an ensemble machine learning algorithm. It uses a meta-learning algorithm to learn how to best combine the predictions from two or more base machine learning algorithms.

The benefit of stacking is that it can harness the capabilities of a range of well-performing models on a classification or regression task and make predictions that have better performance than any single model in the ensemble.

Stacking is an ensemble machine learning algorithm that learns how to best combine the predictions from multiple well-performing machine learning models.

CHAPTER SEVEN

Current Machine Learning Healthcare Applications

Diagnosis in Medical Imaging

Computer vision has been one of the most remarkable breakthroughs, thanks to machine learning and deep learning, and it's a particularly active healthcare application for ML. Microsoft's inner eye initiative (started in 2010) is presently working on image diagnostic tools, and the team has posted a number of videos explaining their developments, including this video on machine learning for image analysis:

Robotic Surgery

The da Vinci robot has gotten the heft of consideration in the mechanical medical procedure space, and some could contend in light of current circumstances. This gadget permits specialists to control dexterous automated appendages to do medical procedures with fine detail and in restricted spaces (and with fewer quakes) than would be conceivable by the human hand alone. Here's a video featuring the fantastic mastery of the Da Vinci robot: While not all mechanical medical procedure methods include AI, a few frameworks use PC vision (helped by AI) to distinguish distances, or a particular body part, (for example, recognizing hair follicles for transplantation on the head, on account of hair transplantation medical procedure). What's more, AI is at times used to consistent the movement and development of automated appendages when taking headings from human regulators.

CHAPTER EIGHT

Machine Learning for IoT HealthCare Applications

Web of Things and Machine Learning (ML) have wide appropriateness in numerous parts of life, medical services are one of them. With the quick turn of events and improvement of the web, the ordinary techniques for patient administration were reduced and replaced with electronic medical care systems. The utilization of IoT innovation offers clinical experts and patients the most present-day clinical gadget climate. IoT things and Machine-Learning are significant in different orders from far away from seeing of the advanced environment to mechanical motorization. Besides, clinical consideration applications are primarily demonstrating interest in IoT thingfulfilments taking into account cost decline, straightforwardly and improving the individual fulfillment of patients. The most recent applications for IoT clinical treatment, researched and as yet dealing with issues in the clinical climate, are required for scholarly, inventions based answers. In explicit, convenient, and implantable IoT model gadgets, are examined for ascertaining the information transmission. Implantable advancements lead to the characteristic replacement of the harmed part of the human body. The making of wearable and implantable medical care body territory network confronted a few difficulties that are delineated in this examination. In this book, an outline of IoT and Machine Learning dependent on medical services care is exhibited in detail, the applications that utilization in medical care by fusing Machine Learning (ML) for the Internet of Things (IoT) are recorded with all issues and difficulties while utilizing this application or gadgets for medical care and their significant use. Additionally, calculations utilized by Machine Learning in IoT for creating gadgets are demonstrated by showing past work and characterized every one of them as indicated by the pre-owned strategy.

Machine Learning Algorithms in IoT

Medicine Box with an android (Health-IoT) application that allows patients and physicians to communicate more closely. A smart medicine box is provided on the proposed platform which warns patients to take their treatment on time. The box has wireless internet connectivity to ensure timely notifications of medicines that are informed with the patient's mobile in the android program. The machine automatically warns the patient so that the correct medication is received at the right time. And if vital signs occur, the pre-configure protector receives SMS warnings. While in their study suggests a method/framework for tracking the medical consumption of patients. It offers frameworks for the dissemination of prescription drugs and the monitoring of the history of prescription. It may be said in this respect that the Internet of Things will give a more customized, preventive, and cooperative type of treatment a new aspect to contemporary healthcare. This investigation provided a live IoT solution for elderly people to monitor and record their patients' vital information and promoting emergency alert systems. The research proposed a way to monitor and assist elderly people with a bracelet that can be connected to the cloud server. It is meant to become a cost-effective wireless networking solution. Open Research Issues and Future Direction for ML and IoT in healthcare. Machine learning is carefully related to mathematical comparison, to decision-making based totally on modern evidence, and forecasts located thru past knowledge. In the case of patient monitoring, the ML-based method can consider the circumstance according to the data collection. Learning datasets play an essential position in accurately predicting the new problem's future trend. The statistics series can be distorted regularly and not special to a wide range of situations. Noisy data, messy data, and incomplete facts will lead to much less chance of analysis and recommendation on health detection and prediction. In the case of controlling sleep and heart problems, the patterns and routines of sleep can range by way of person, age, and health. Therefore, a whole list of the cases of sleep cycles cannot be obtained, which may also lead to inaccurate PH calculations. If IoT and ML are used, allows PH, for detection, estimation, and alerting of the patient, the laptop would possibly need to determine. Any

circumstances can also lead to a mistake of an ML-based judgment, and it is tough to point out that a precise choice is made. Few crashes have passed off because of a self reliant car's incorrect decision. The essential difficulty is how to interpret a machine's choice. Disadvantages can preclude the use of ML in PH insensitive use such as custom medicine.

Issues and challenges

Customized electronic medical therapy is no longer open to challenges and weaknesses. It takes into account the essential issues of IoT and ML. This provides an example in which an elderly character uses a Personalized Healthcare (PH) gadget primarily based on a sensor. The sensor gathers different details, for example, heart rate, Environmental supplement, blood sugar, pressure, etc. The data is processed for use via the participating parties. The database additionally uses some computer education algorithms to interpret the facts obtained to decide the danger factor for patients, improve their health, and advocate conceivable strategies on this groundwork. The primary things and challenges around IoT and ML in PH solutions are the volume of information produced via the sensors is massive. The retrieval of the right information from the data gathered is a challenge. This initiative entails the introduction of an algorithm that can extract patterns in amassed records from physique sensor networks. Major research scopes arise in the vicinity of laptop mastering and sampling algorithms. In view of the fact that computer-intensive techniques are being held back, the efficiency of Real-Time Response is a location of development. Optimizing the quantity of data transmission is a count number of concern. Privatization of computing, with extra and greater IoT-enabled computers, one-point computing would create a hindrance in community power. The algorithm needs to be shared and the parallel processing of the undertaking stage wants to be accomplished. Computational and resource allocation algorithms are areas of good sized research significance in this field. The battery used in IoT gadgets is one of the main issues, so it might also no longer be handy to cost these devices. Generally, discharges to a back-end processor and saves battery capacity, which would otherwise have been sufficient for internal computing, resolves this issue.

CHAPTER NINE

CONCLUSION

The objective of this book was to consolidate existing research on the Internet of Things in health care and related topics that allow for constructing a body of knowledge. The long-anticipated IoT revolution in healthcare is already underway, as the examples in this book demonstrate. They continue to resolve the urgent need for safe, efficient care as new use cases emerge. Meanwhile, the automation and machine-to-machine communication building blocks of the Internet of Things continue to be created. With the addition of the service layer, the IoT infrastructure is complete. End-to-end processing and networking technologies for IoT-driven healthcare are hallmarks of this movement. The field is still in its early stages and in order to mature, IoT and health care researchers should come together by proposing effective analytic methods. Healthcare is one of the fastest-growing segments of the economy today; more people need care, and it is becoming more expensive. Government health-care spending has reached an all-time high, while the critical need for better patient-physician relationships has become apparent. Big data and machine intelligence technologies have the potential to transform care and lower costs for both patients and providers. Several companies and organizations have already taken the first steps in this direction. This aided in the transition to patient-centered, evidence-based treatment. The information is already available; we just need to figure out how to access it. Furthermore, the system's learning is heavily reliant on the data and algorithms available to categorize data into specific classes through supervised or uncontrolled learning. People make bad decisions, and we humans often rely on evidence to make decisions. We also make decisions based on our feelings, but computers do not. Overcoming IoT and ML weaknesses will increase the health of the client more. This book focused to discuss the general view on IoT and ML which are applied in the health care system, the application used for personalized health care and demonstrated some other related works and their opinions. We humans have the ability to choose based on our moral beliefs, global observation, political and religious values, and identity. These variables will be used in the data collection used to train computers to make decisions. It's also a challenge to make sure that the data collected for learning is free of machine biases as much as possible.

9 798886 841022

Printed by Libri Plureos GmbH in Hamburg,
Germany